How to Say "I Love You"

How to Say "I Love You"

by Gene Accas and
John H. Eckstein

AN ESSANDESS SPECIAL EDITION
NEW YORK

HOW TO SAY "I LOVE YOU"

SBN 671-10311-3

Published by *Essandess Special Editions,*
a division of Simon & Schuster, Inc.,
630 Fifth Avenue, New York, N.Y. 10020,
and on the same day in Canada
by Simon & Schuster of Canada, Ltd.,
Richmond Hill, Ontario.

Printed in the U.S.A.

Acknowledgments

For arrangements made with various authors and publishing houses where copyrighted material was permitted to be reprinted, and for the courtesy extended by them, the following acknowledgments are gratefully made. All possible care has been taken to trace the ownership of every selection included and to make full acknowledgment for its use. If any errors have accidentally occurred, they will be corrected in subsequent editions, provided notification is sent to the publisher.

Prentice-Hall, Inc., for permission to use material from *The Human Side of Successful Communication* by Robert E. Moore, copyright © 1961 by Prentice-Hall, Inc.

FOR SANDRA AND ANITA—
who each inspired us to greater
affectionate imagination.

The Authors

Foreword

WHETHER you are single or married, young or old, male or female . . .

You may, as most people do, find it difficult to express affection—you may need help.

It is through the little things, tender things, thoughtful, inexpressibly precious things that boy and girl, man and woman, can express love for each other.

This guidebook, in easy-to-find, easy-to-say, easy-to-do expressions of affection, will help you convey warmth and love in ways that are simple and meaningful.

One can say "I care" in many, many ways: on anniversaries, holidays, or just special, personal days; by loving words, tender tokens, affectionate gestures; by do-it-yourself gifts and compose-it-yourself poems and songs.

In addition to hundreds of ideas which say "I love you," this book is filled with well-known and little-known quotations about love (use these, too), each of which says a special something about love.

Ask yourself, "How can *I* express myself more affectionately and more often?

What shall I wear to convey affection?

What dishes shall I order that can convey tenderness?

What beverages shall I order, or serve at home?

What music shall I sing, or play?

What shall I give?"

And most important, "What, where and when shall I say it?"

Are you a bachelor, a career girl, or a teenager? Are

you married, divorced, or widowed? Do you live in a big city or are you a suburbanite? . . . Successful professional or clerical worker, or just starting on a factory job?

In short, this is intended to be a complete reference book for anyone who, anytime, anywhere, wants to say to someone else, "I care about you."

Gene Accas
John H. Eckstein

Contents

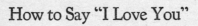

How to Say "I Love You"

IF YOU ARE

female and feminine ...

single ... whether teeny-bopper,

girl, woman, or grandmother ...

This is your special

love section.

IT began with Adam and Eve.

Ever since, love has made the world go 'round. Song and story echo and re-echo the importance of love. Love is the one emotion that sets man apart from all other life on earth.

Love can be defined a thousand ways. Some equate it to God. Others say it is caring more for someone than oneself.

We can love. We do love. The difficulty comes in *expressing* love. Most people are shy, or reticent, or simply don't have the imagination to convey their affection often and adequately enough.

In more romantic centuries of the past, when one was in love, personal communication seemed to have been easier. In today's taut world, it is somehow more difficult to convey love, even with our greater freedom and freedom of expression.

As a result, there isn't enough communication of love to meet the need—for we all not only need love, we need to *know* we are loved.

Make a Book on Love

Get a large, blank scrapbook.

In it paste photos, newspaper clippings, souvenir programs, postcards, and so on, to make a chronology of your love and life together.

When it has a number of items in it, give it (on some special day—birthday, anniversary, or such) to your loved one.

Every now and again, add some new items, and even new pages, to your scrapbook of love.

> *Two souls with but a single thought,*
> *Two hearts that beat as one.*
> —VON MÜNCH-BELLINGHAUSEN

Love by Repetition

Use a bulletin board, a blackboard, or a plain sheet of paper. On it write "I love you" 100 times in your own handwriting, as if it were a grammar school "penmanship lesson."

Do this whenever the spirit moves you. It can't be done too often.

I want not only to be loved, but to be told that I am loved.
The realm of silence is large enough beyond the grave.
—GEORGE ELIOT

Your Language of Love

Choose one or two (not too many, or the intimate effect is spoiled) special love words or phrases.

These can be silly words . . . nonsense words . . . or personal "code words." They must belong to just you two. The words will mean something special, only to you, not to anyone else.

They can be your own words for "kiss" . . . "loving" . . . "I can't wait" . . . "I need you" . . . or any one of a thousand expressions of love and affection.

Use these words, in public or in private, as your special language of love, to convey the "one-ness" that exists between the two of you.

It's love, it's love that
makes the world go round.

Post Your Love

Every city, town, or hamlet has local scenic postcards. Bookstores, drugstores, travel terminals, lots of places carry them, at five cents each, or six for 25¢.

Buy a batch. Every now and again, address one to your love with a simple little affectionate message on it.

And don't forget the special "postal signal of love" (how you place the stamp, descriptive words in the address, and so on).

Be Natural-ly Lovely

Styles and fads come and go. Women are women, and will always be. It's just possible that he likes you as you are: natural—a simple hairstyle, without eye-liner and shadow or mini-dress—without the things that are "now."

Find out. And if this is the case, be natural once in a while (maybe on weekends, or just around the neighborhood).

This may mean newly washed hair, slightly curled . . . it may mean no make-up other than lipstick . . . it may mean a casual sweater and skirt. If so, fine.

If it shows you love him specially . . . and he will know it does . . . just be natural from time to time.

Ask what is sweetness of thy kiss—
Ask of thyself what beauty is.
                    —P. J. BAILEY,
                    Festus

Love Should Be Timely

Disagreements are the enemy of love. And no matter how much you love, or may be loved, this applies to you.

One major source of friction between lovers is lateness. So be punctual! When you say ten minutes, make it ten, not twelve or fifteen minutes.

When you say, "I'll meet you at 7:30," be there at half-past seven, not eight or nine. Respect your sweetheart, for this means respecting your love's time, patience, and emotions.

> *With all thy faults, I love thee still.*
> —WILLIAM COWPER,
> *The Task,* II

Wear a Banner of Love

Unquestionably, there is a special accessory you have that was either given to you by your lover, or is a favorite of his.

If so, wear that banner of love on those days you want especially to convey a message of affection.

(Girls, this applies to a scarf, pin, hat, or some other accessory he is particularly fond of.)

Frozen Love Assets

Most dime stores, in their notions or toy departments, have dozens of charms and trinkets. Buy little toys, plastic letters, souvenirs of many kinds—but they must be small.

Make sure you wash the item well in soap and water. Partially fill an ice cube tray, and place or "float" the item in one of the compartments. After the "base" is frozen, fill the tray up to the proper level and freeze again.

Use these special cubes as the coolers in the cocktails or soft drinks that you prepare and serve your sweetheart when you want to remind him that you love him.

⚬⚬⚬⚬⚬

A Love-ly Knit

Can you knit?

Why not make a pair of socks for that special guy? Include your and his initials . . . a pair of entwined hearts . . . some other special design (or even a love saying) into the uppers of the socks.

The "Knitty-Gritty" of Love

If you can't knit, you might find a friend or relative who can (or, if you can afford it, someone who knits commercially). Have a pair of sweaters made in the same color scheme and, if it suits you both, the same style and shape.

Include in the design special words, initials, or shapes. Perhaps a pair of doves has special meaning for you two . . . or a loving cup . . . a pair of riding boots—use whatever symbolizes your affection.

❧❧❧

Picture Your Love

Have your portrait painted in oils.

Yes, it can be done, and for less than a fortune.

Many national magazines, especially the women's magazines, carry advertisements of artists' companies that will make lovely, lifelike oil portraits just from photographs.

Find such an advertisement. Send them several photos. When the painting is finished, have it framed, and give it to your lover on a very special day, to become a tribute to your love.

Love-Town, U. S. A.

The ZIP codes of three towns in Iowa are as follows: Floyd, 50435 . . . George, 51237 . . . Imogene, 51645.

There is a ZIP Code Directory which you'll find in most post offices. Or perhaps the place where you work has one. This directory contains, alphabetically by state, the names and ZIP codes of thousands of U.S. cities and towns.

Most likely, there is a place with the same name as your loved one's, or perhaps there is a place that is romantically important to you both.

You can have a love letter postmarked from that special place, simply by enclosing it (with proper address and postage) in a second envelope; then mail the envelope to the postmaster of the town and request that he mail, locally, the letter you want your sweetheart to receive.

All Love Wears a Smile

The gentlest sign there is, is a smile. Smiling conveys peace and tranquility, and affection.

This love thought is simple and to the point—smile warmly, lovingly, and often. Tell your loved one, with your smile, "I love you now and always."

If we spend our lives in loving, we will have no leisure to complain, or to feel unhappy.

—JOSEPH JOUBERT

Starry-Eyed Love

See it in the stars!

Is your special person interested in astrology? Millions are. More likely than not, in the city in which you live, there is a "professional astrologist," someone who casts and reads horoscopes.

Contact that person, and ask her to make a special horoscope reading for the love life of your loved one. (Make sure the horoscope is favorable to you!)

Then, have the horoscope mailed so that it is delivered on a personal, propitious day, and sit back and wait for the "backlash of affection."

Where Love Is At

There is more to the world as seen through the eyes of flower children and "hippies" than just daydreams. One of the principal articles of faith is love. And since that single word has been equated with God . . . and has lasted a million years . . . they may have something.

The flower people have a visible symbol of love—beads. You may think these strange or "way out," but really, the beads are a simple, declarative statement. They say "I love you and the world."

Think what your loved one would say if you presented him with a string of love beads. Anyhow, try it!

Love Preserved

Flowers are nature's purest expression of joy!

If you love flowers (and who doesn't!), you'll love to have them preserved. So, keep the flowers (a nosegay, a bouquet, or a corsage) of a special occasion, and dry them. There are several simple ways of doing this, and your local library has at least one book that will show you how.

When the flowers are dried, have them framed, with a simple handwritten notation of the date and the occasion.

There are a number of things that can be done with dried flowers—incorporated as part of a shadow-box display . . . mounted under plastic to decorate a photo album cover—but whatever you do with your memento of love, your loving thoughts will keep the flowers "fresh."

> *Flower o' the clove,*
> *All the Latin I construe is "amo,"*
> *I love!*
>
> —ROBERT BROWNING,
> *Fra Lippo Lippi*

Love on a Date

Think about reminding your lover of days special to you both.

Buy a pocket calendar (it can be inexpensive, or can cost $10 if bound in fine leather).

But before giving it, go through the book carefully, and fill in little personal notes, days to remember, things to do, love notes and thoughts of the days to come which the love you share makes special.

cᴏᴄᴏᴄᴏ

For Love and Money

He has a wallet (or money clip), but more precious than money is a sweetheart. So take a good, small photo (preferably in color), have it laminated (sandwiched between sheets of clear, protective plastic), and slip it in with his money in his wallet or clip. In addition, you might think of signing the picture, with a love message!

A "Write" Way to Love

Most people have a nickname, or are known to intimates by a diminutive of a first name.

You can make a hit with your loved one by getting inexpensive "fun" stationery imprinted with his nickname.

Write a love note on one sheet, put it into an envelope, and place it on top of the package when presenting it.

❧❧❧❧

Win Your Letter in Love

Colleges award varsity letters (the initial of the school) to outstanding athletes. These are attached to either pullover or cardigan sweaters.

You can find a store that sells initial letters, and you probably own (or can purchase) an appropriate sweater.

Put the two together, and some day soon, blossom out in a sweater adorned with the initial of your sweetheart's first name.

Let him (and anybody) figure out how you won your letter.

Call for Love

There are public places (hotel lobbies, bowling alleys, sports arenas) where paging is done—in person or over the public address system.

On an occasion when your sweetheart is at one of these places without you, have him paged. When he picks up the message (in an envelope if it's an in-person place for paging; on the phone, if it isn't), the message is very simple: "I called to say I.L.Y."

⁂

Love Is a Snap

Girls, give your man an identification bracelet that snaps open to show your picture. (But don't force it on him if that kind of jewelry is out of character!)

⁂

Signal of Love

It's an old Polynesian custom. . . .
Women in the lovely islands of the South Pacific wear
a flower (usually a hibiscus) in their hair as a signal:

—Blossom over left ear: married or spoken for.
—Blossom over right ear: available and looking.

Try this yourself, or work out another "code" . . . ear-
rings, scarf, handkerchief, or any accessory that will
convey your mood to your sweetheart.
It makes sense—you can tell him, without words,
whether or not you are feeling affectionate or passive.
Try it, it works!

In her first passion, woman loves her lover;
In all others, all she loves is love.
　　　　　　　　　　—LORD BYRON,
　　　　　　　　　　Don Juan, III

ᴄᴠᴢᴄᴠᴢᴄᴠᴢ

IF YOU ARE

male ... available ... dashing

and dashing about ... Look

through the next few pages to

find some pin-pointed

love ideas for you.

It is often more difficult for men than for women to express love, affection, tenderness, call it what you will.

Why is this so? Because, basically, we are shy about exposing our emotions. Somehow, we think it "weak," "unmanly," "mixed up," or contrive some other allegedly undesirable excuse not to tell someone that we care for her deeply. That her happiness and well-being are important. That her being happy multiplies our happiness. That when she is gloomy or downcast, we are, too.

What nonsense!

Think of the times you have "loved the whole world." How weak was that? How unnatural did it feel?

This book of ideas—some wildly romantic, some passionate, some gaily carefree—is meant to help you say "I love you" more often, by word, thought, and action, to the one person in the world who means most to you.

Use these ideas freely. And let your own imagination, your own personal likes and tastes guide you to express your love in your own way.

Be a Wild Lover

Wild flowers have said "love" since time began.

Nature's loveliest expression is in flowers. And in nearly every place that isn't covered by concrete and asphalt, there are wild flowers. When you find some, pick them—a small bunch will do—and bring them to your sweetheart.

It was good—very good—for your father and grandfather, your mother and grandmother. Why not you?

Say something very simple, very sweet, very "you" when you present the flowers. She'll love you and remember the day.

Make Your Love Charm-ing

Start a charm bracelet.

First, give her the chain, and one important (very personal, meaningful) charm.

On special days thereafter add other charms, each one dedicated to "us" . . . "love" . . . and so on. Each time you give a charm, make sure it is accompanied by a love note or card, expressing your sentiments.

എസ

A Study in Love

You may need help occasionally to articulate your thoughts of love. Here are two dandy sources:

Pocket Book of Quotations (75¢)—more than 3,000 appropriate quotations, neatly divided into categories. Look one up that suits your love and write it or say it often.

Roget's Thesaurus (comes in various editions, some very inexpensive). This is a kind of "reverse dictionary," which gives you multiple words, synonyms, antonyms for various subjects. An example of its richness: Under "affection" there are some 200 items.

There are other source books to which you can refer for ideas on how to express your affection.

Do a little research—it will reward you handsomely with your loved one.

Speak Low, When You Speak Love

There is a great deal of psychological evidence that one sure way to de-escalate an argument is to progressively lower your voice. It is also pretty well established that the favorite word in most people's vocabulary is their own name.

So, as an open-secret way of saying "I love you," try whispering your loved one's name often.

> *Doubt thou stars are fire;*
> *Doubt that the sun doth move;*
> *Doubt truth to be a liar;*
> *But never doubt I love.*
> —WILLIAM SHAKESPEARE,
> *Hamlet,* II, 2

Love à la Carte

Today you can choose from a huge selection of posters, balloons, ashtrays, coffee cups, scarves, and buttons with "hip" sayings.

There are even some very attractive love posters available. Next time she's out, attach one of these (maybe it reads "Love is sweeping the nation") to the front door before she comes home.

It's a unique, thoughtful way of saying "I love you."

Chalk One Up for Love

Kid stuff is fun stuff. You can't mail your loved one a piece of sidewalk with chalked love words on it; nor a section of fence; nor a carved tree trunk. But any stationery store has black drawing paper (the kind children use in art class) and you can buy a pack of it.

Get some chalk, too, and write your special love message on a sheet. For instance . . . "John loves Mary" . . . or "I can't count the ways I.L.Y."

Mail the message home or to the office—somewhere your loved one isn't expecting to be wooed.

To love for the sake of being loved is human,
but to love for the sake of loving is angelic.
—ALPHONSE DE LAMARTINE,
Graziella, IV

Smooth and Love·ly

Sure, shaving is a tedious bore. And no matter how close-shaven you are today, you'll have stubble tomorrow, and have to do it all over.

But you should, as a mark of affection and respect, shave every day. And on special occasions, you might even shave in the evening—and tell her why.

Tape Your Love

Do you own a tape recorder? If not, surely a friend must have one.

Get a book of love poems and record some that you think appropriate for your loved one. Make it a real poetry reading.

You might even substitute her name in place of one you'll find in a poem. Then present her with the tape on a special occasion; or, you might send it as a "living letter" when you're away on a long business trip.

Love on the Telephone

Call up your dearest.

Do it from office to home . . . at whatever hour of the day. Say these three magic words—that's all:

"I Love You!"

Hang up. End of conversation. Start, probably, of a whole new attitude.

There are many people who would never have been in love if they had never heard love spoken of.
—LA ROCHEFOUCAULD,
Maxims, 136

Love in the Open

Come spring or summer, doesn't your city have outdoor concerts? Along the river bank . . . in the park . . . somewhere?

Can you think of a more romantic setting? Music under the stars, and your sweetheart.

Plan such a romantic outing, and to make it an extra special event, bring along a bottle of chilled wine, or even champagne, and glasses for just the two of you.

> *Come live with me and be my love,*
> *And we will all the pleasures prove*
> *That hills and valleys, dale and field,*
> *Or woods, or steepy mountains yield.*
> —CHRISTOPHER MARLOWE,
> *The Passionate Shepherd to His Love*

Love in the Cards

Greeting cards are big business, and fortunately for those with considerate instincts, there is now an infinite variety of cards for every occasion and for no occasion at all.

You can demonstrate your love and thoughtfulness by sending a card once in a while for no reason except sheer friendliness . . . a card that says, "How nice it is to know you," or, if on a business trip, an "I miss you" card.

Go wild and even send a Valentine's Day card in July!

Love on the Aisle

Kid stuff?

Never. It's an old American custom (as old as the 1940's, anyway). What are we talking about? A drive-in movie, of course!

Plan an excursion there soon, just the two of you. It really doesn't matter terribly what the feature is, or how bad it is.

What does matter is the two of you in a car, with dim lights and popcorn bags, being very, very affectionate.

How about tomorrow night?

The theologian is right. Why not admit it? More than anything else the world needs love.

—SEBASTIAN DEGRAZIA

Sing a Happy Love Tune

Whistle, sing, hum, or learn to pick out a simple tune on a musical instrument. But make it a special song, your love song, a song that belongs to the two of you.

When there is an opportunity, even if there is a crowd about, say you love her by making music . . . singing, whistling, humming, or playing.

For Latin Lovers

Is she a student of the classics? She may not be, but there are still those who study Latin, and even ancient Greek.

There is probably a college or university near your home. A polite, persuasive note to the Chairman of the Classics Department asking for the Latin (or Greek) "spell-out" of a personal "love diploma" should bring a helpful response. You can compose the words in English that you want translated.

When the translation does come back, take it to a local sign painter (they can usually do pretty fine hand-lettering) and ask him to "fake" a diploma for you. Have it framed, so that it can be hung in her den, living room, or other appropriate room, along with other family trophies.

It's an unusual way of saying, "You've graduated from the school of advanced affection, and have won your diploma as my sweetheart."

Remember, the wording should bear some resemblance to the form of a college diploma, but it should be converted to reflect your personal relationship.

Love conquers all; let us yield to Love.
(Omnia vincit Amor; et nos cedamus Amori.)
—VIRGIL,
Eclogues, X

ↄ♥ↄ♥ↄ♥ↄ

A Good Time for Love

Here's a "timely" idea. Today, there are all sorts of novelty clocks (and they aren't too expensive) on the market. Mostly, they are transistorized, battery-operated models, with "kookie" faces. Some have Roman numerals, others Hebrew numbers, still others have just the letters L-O-V-E (in the 12-3-6-9 positions, respectively).

Such a clock is great, and there is an even more personal way to use it as a love token. Take it to a good sign painter and have him letter in appropriate letters or words for the numbers 1 through 12. You might use the date of your engagement or meeting, properly spaced. Or, it could be a message such as "JJS adores MLS."

Be inventive. The message will get through!

ↄ♥ↄ♥ↄ♥ↄ

Give Your Love a Future

Is your sweetheart fascinated by the future? Most people are.

Why not "fix" the future? There are probably gypsy tea rooms, or "readers and advisors" in some nearby locality.

Take a trip to the place and arrange with the local fortune-teller to make a reading of something that you want to have told to your sweetheart. (You'll probably have to tip the gypsy in advance, but undoubtedly she'll be willing to cooperate fully).

After all, all the world (including gypsies) loves a lover.

There is nothing half so sweet in life
As love's young dream.
> —THOMAS MOORE,
> *Love's Young Dream*

If love were what the rose is,
And I were like the leaf,
Our lives would grow together
In sad or singing weather.
> —A. C. SWINBURNE,
> *A Match*

A Fortune of Love

Nearly every town of any size has one or more Chinese restaurants. And most people like Chinese food.

Next time you plan to eat a Chinese meal, do a little planning and preparation. Make up a slip of paper that has a special love saying on it—something that is especially meaningful to the two of you.

Write it (or type it) on a very little slip of tissue (the kind used for carbon copies of office correspondence). Take the slip to the restaurant before you go there for your meal.

Ask the proprietor to slip the message into a fortune cookie, and make sure that particular cookie is served to your loved one as dessert.

Get a Lovebird

Yes, we mean a *lovebird*. Start with a pet store. See the proprietor and tell him you'll buy a talking bird (parakeet, parrot, mynah—any kind that can be taught to speak)—if he will teach it to say, "I love you, —— (the name of your sweetheart)."

Then, after the bird has learned his line, and only then, you make a present to your sweetheart. She will be pleased!

A Heart Full of Love

In medieval times, people used to believe that love came from the heart. (Certainly, in passionate circumstances, the heartbeat speeds up.)

But forgetting the fact or fiction of the anatomy of love, there is no question that the heart shape still symbolizes "love" for most people.

So surround your loved one with heart-shaped symbols. You'll find dozens of them in every kind of store: plates, lockets, picture frames, paperweights, fabric designs—you name it.

The point is to make it a personal, just-you-two communication. Every time you find something that is heart-shaped, buy it for your loved one. ("Squirrel" it away for an occasion, and present this symbol of love to your sweetheart.)

❦❦❦

Love Telegraphy

Whatever is very personal, whatever says "love" to just the two of you, whatever is just your own—this is the way to communicate *your* love.

There are many things you can do—silently speak "I love you," so that your sweetheart can see your lips form the words . . . gently stroke the back of her neck while dancing . . . an under-the-table pressure of your knee against hers . . . a slow, meaningful wink between you . . . a hundred other ways, one of which should be just yours.

Reserve the special love "telegraphy" for times and places that make you want to say "I love you"—in the midst of people, after a misunderstanding, or in places where it's difficult to speak aloud. It will be meaningful simply because it's meant just for her.

A Living Love Token

Next to babies, everybody loves puppies and kittens. And, if your loved one loves pets, nothing will make a longer, more lasting, more loving token than a kitten or puppy, given on a special day, and named (by either of you) for something very near, very personal, and very meaningful to the two of you.

Lockets and Love-a-liers

Fashions these days are made by individuals. Almost anything goes. Certainly, women can wear lockets, or lavaliers, or special "old-fashioned" rings. But you are interested in some piece of jewelry that opens—that has a place for a picture, your picture.

Most likely you'll find one of these personal items in a thrift shop, a rummage shop, or even in a "used jewelry" shop. You might find one in a regular store. You want something that suits her personality and the kind of clothes she wears. Then you should have the photo carefully fitted in. (Better have a photographer's shop make the reduction to fit.)

A Love Serenade

"Say it with music . . ." goes the charming Irving Berlin ballad. Why not? You can have your sweetheart serenaded with guitar or accordion music (perhaps a violin), or with a choral group.

It should not be difficult to find the group—in the yellow pages of your phone directory, at the local college or university where there are music departments, or where there is a fraternity or sorority with a prize-winning glee club.

Make the arrangements—it shouldn't cost too much, especially if they are amateurs—and have the serenade take place one evening, unexpectedly!

Love is never lost. If not reciprocated it will flow back and soften and purify the heart.

—WASHINGTON IRVING

The Sweet-ness of Love

What's your favorite dessert or candy?
What's hers?
Whatever it is, make it a point of ordering, serving, or buying that particular sweet and making it yours on special days and occasions. And every time you share the sweet taste, make sure that you convey the thought of "sweetheart" to your love.

Be Neatly in Love

Be fastidious. In today's world of scientific miracles, there is no excuse for any personal offense. The surest way to kill a romance is to be unsavory—to offend with any personal uncleanliness or odor.

There are deodorants, deodorant soaps, mouthwashes, and breath sprays. Whatever might offend (and even loved ones may not be brave enough to tell you), you can overcome the problem with a simple visit to your drugstore, and regular care thereafter.

Make a Love Call

"Call me at six on the dot. . . . "

So goes a line in a popular love song. Why not borrow the idea? Call your special person just to say "I love you," but do it at a special time of the day.

Call at home (or at her office, store, or other place of work) and always just make a brief, loving remark. Don't have a long conversation, and don't talk about anything else. Let other news or problems or errands wait for another call. Just tell your loved one of the affection you feel.

How to Click in Love

Do you know someone who is a good amateur photographer? Of course you do!

Have a whole bunch of candid photos taken of you. Choose the best single one and have it enlarged (say to 8 by 10 inches). Carefully autograph it, with some special sentiment, and have it framed.

Make it a personal gift on a personal day.

Then take all the other poses and have them made into an album. Write a particular note or message under (or opposite) each one, and make this a follow-up gift on the very next special day.

> *To see her is to love her,*
> *And love but her forever;*
> *For Nature made her what she is,*
> *And never made anither!*
> —ROBERT BURNS,
> *O, Saw Ye Bonnie Lesley*

ↄ৶৶ↄ৶৶ↄ৶৶

How to Seal Your Love

In the olden days, special letters—of love, or of royal import—were sealed.

So, buy some sealing wax (most variety and sundry stores carry it, and certainly stationery and business supply stores do) and get it in a distinctive color.

Go to a jeweler's, and purchase an inexpensive "seal" or signet ring with your initial. Then, whenever you write your loved one, don't seal the envelope the usual way, but stamp the colored wax with your own special love seal.

❧❧❧

The Language of Love

Learn to say "I love you" in a foreign language. Then, whenever there is a "trigger" for it (the name of that country is mentioned in the news, you see a picture of it in a magazine, or any other reminders) say to your loved one in French, *"Je t'aime,"* or say "I love you" in whatever other foreign tongue you've chosen (call on the phone if you're away).

(At the end of this guidebook, you will find the words for "I love you" in some thirty languages, as well as a guide to pronunciation.)

Love in Bloom

Send a barrage of flowers.

Make a "deal" with a local florist. Have him deliver a single, lovely rose (or whatever favorite flower your love has) with a simple bud vase on "the first day."

This can be a birthday, anniversary, or other special day. Then, at periodic intervals have a single flower delivered—no card, no words, nothing—and let the flower speak for you. (She'll know who sent it.)

Write a Love Song!

Right! And if you don't have any musical talent, don't let that stand in your way. It can be done simply.

First, try the local music school or high school, or the music department of a nearby college. (If these aren't available, look up a local piano teacher in the phone book, and contact him.)

Tell the "musician" very simply that you want a song dedicated to your loved one. Sit down before you make the visit, and enumerate all the special, wonderful things about her. Bring the list with you. Ask the musician if he can (or if he can suggest someone else who can) compose a simple song called —— (the name of your girl). In most cases, he will be glad to, for a nominal fee. Have him tape the song for you, and present it!

Love Potion

Concoct a drink, and name it for your loved one.

Talk to a bartender. Tell him your love's favorite wine, liquor, or even soft drink.

Work out something new with him. (Make sure you taste it to see that it's palatable.) Then, next time you're out, order the "Nancy" or "Barbara," and since the bartender won't know its ingredients, you tell him.

While he's making it, tell your partner that the drink was invented just for her.

I will reveal to you a love potion, without medicine, without herbs, without any witch's magic. If you want to be loved then love.

—HECATON OF RHODES

Underscore Your Love

Get hold of a copy of your beloved's favorite book (or one she is currently reading). Go through it in advance, and underscore (or make marginal notations) throughout the text.

Use a special, transparent, colored Magic Marker (make sure it's transparent ink). Highlight passages, sentences, words, and phrases that tell her how you love her, and her alone.

Carve Out Your Love

Be a kid!

Find an old tree. On it carve your initials, and her initials. If possible, frame them with a heart, then put an arrow through it! Visit your tree every once in a while.

Make Love a Feast

Quietly, through observation, questioning, and experimentation, find out your loved one's favorite dishes—appetizer . . . entrée . . . salad . . . dessert . . . wine—everything.

Make sure the courses "go together," and are compatible! Then, on a special occasion, preferably at a special restaurant, *you* do the ordering in advance by visiting the restaurant the day before, or by telephone. Make a point of saying that the meal is your "love feast."

Do it again—on all your personal, special days, have your own "love feast."

IF YOU ARE

sweethearts ... lovers ... that

wondrous combination closest to

heaven — two people in love ...

Then turn to the loving thoughts

that have been compiled just

for you two.

THIS guide was written to help those who love to express affection toward one another.

Love is an emotion that functions like a muscle. It grows and expands with exercise and use. It can atrophy and wither with inactivity. When the feeling moves you, let the words come out, let your emotions off their leash.

Do it. Try it. Say it. Mean it. "I love you."

You'll be stronger, happier, richer for it. By the way, so will someone else. And the two of you, after all, are a very important part of the world!

Loving and being loved is a dream. *Knowing* you are loved is the reality. Let your loved one know it.

A Profile of Love

Be corny, be old-fashioned, be loving.

The silhouette is as outdated as the buggy whip. But it is a lovely reminder of gentler times, when the rush and pressures of the twentieth century weren't anyone's nightmares.

At many county fairs, in many art schools, the almost-forgotten art of silhouette-cutting is still practiced.

If you think your sweetheart would like the thought and gift, find such an artist.

He'll need you and some profile photos of your sweetheart. From the "live" and the "paper" people, he can make for you a twin silhouette—the two of you side by side, like some fairy-tale prince and princess.

It's a lovely gift!

You say to me-wards your affection's strong;
Pray love me little, so you love me long.
—ROBERT HERRICK

Make a Record of Your Love

Go to a recording studio. Before you do, write out what you want to say. But make sure you say what is in your heart; don't just read it off. Make it sincere, earnest, conversational.

Cut a record or make a tape recording. Don't hold back; the recording can be just as personal and intimate as "pillow talk."

Present your verbal love letter to your loved one on a special day—perhaps the anniversary of your first meeting. And don't hesitate to add to her "record collection" as often as you like.

A little while she strove, and much repented,
And whispering "I will ne'er consent"—consented.
                                        —LORD BYRON,
                                            Don Juan, I

∽∾∿∽

A Touch of Love

What caress pleases your sweetheart?

Is it a gentle squeeze of the hand? Stroking the top of her head? Gently rubbing her back?

Whatever caress is most pleasurable—and it need not, in fact should not, be erotic—reserve this way of conveying your affection for private, relaxed moments.

Make it your caress. Show your tenderness in this special way as often as you both feel it.

A Love-ly Dream

A hundred songs have been written about dreams, and dreams are the stuff of which many lives and loves are made.

The idea here is to make a habit of "dreaming together." There is nothing likely to bring the two of you closer together than sharing a dream. Maybe it's a trip to some far-off place (and it doesn't matter that you may never really go there); perhaps it's a home that you both want, or a sports car, or a mink. Whatever it is, set apart some dreaming time, and just the two of you talk about, elaborate on, embroider, dream big about something you both want.

There's no harm in daydreaming, or evening dreaming, or anytime dreaming. It's a way to intertwine your wishes, and it costs nothing.

It's a Love-ly Day Today

Pick a special day (one that means something to you both) . . . the day you first met . . . became engaged . . . first kissed . . . and make it into an annual (or even monthly) occasion.

Every anniversary, do something special to commemorate "your day."

❧❧❧

Quote I Love You Unquote

Buy a copy of *Bartlett's Familiar Quotations,* available in paperback for $1.45.

Leaf through it. Choose several quotations that are especially meaningful to you and your loved one.

Copy these on little sheets of paper or index cards. Leave a few among your sweetheart's personal effects (tucked in between handkerchiefs, inside a purse or wallet, in record shelves, with pots and pans, in favorite books, and so on).

You'll be pleasantly surprised at how finding one of these love messages can make a sunny day sunnier, and turn a gloomy day into a pleasant one.

Love Is a Tree

Buy a house plant, one without flowers. Make it into a "love tree."

Before giving it, tie or tape little nonsense gifts and love notes to the leaves.

For example: a charm that says something special, a token tie-tack, a single cuff link, or anything small. And put on the love tree two or three short notes that say "I love you," in these and other words.

From time to time, and especially when there is "no occasion," refresh the tree—re-offer it—by putting on a new little trinket, and a little note as well.

❧❧❧

Write a Love Poem

You can't? Of course you can!

Start with something easy. A couplet: two short sentences or phrases ending in words that rhyme. Get an inexpensive rhyming dictionary. Study it in private. Surprise your loved one by writing a special "To —— (her name)" poem yourself. Later on, as you become more sure of yourself, try a short poem in blank verse (that doesn't have to rhyme!).

Deliver it (or give it appropriately) on Valentine's Day or your anniversary.

This Love Thought Should Click

Picture this. Today nearly everyone has, or has access to, a camera.

Our thought here is to use your camera to record the places that mean love to the two of you. Start with a picture of the place you first met—a friend's house, or the beach, perhaps. Continue to record your dating, your courtship, your engagement, with pictures of the places and things that tell the story of your love.

Have them group-framed, by making a large montage in one great big frame. Or make an album of love, and give it to your love, with love.

She is not fair to outward view
As many maidens be:
Her loveliness I never knew
Until she smiled on me.
*—*HARTLEY COLERIDGE,
Song

❧❧❧

Three Hundred and Sixty-Five Days of Love

"How do I love thee, let me count the ways . . ."
This famous sonnet by Elizabeth Barrett Browning
suggests the ways—365 of them.

At the start of a year, buy a diary. Every day, enter
a short, simple statement of love in it. At the start of
the following year (or better still, on New Year's Eve,
when kisses and vows are exchanged), give the 365
"ways I love thee," in the completed diary, to your
sweetheart.

*To love is to find pleasure in the happiness of
the person loved.*

—GOTTFRIED WILHELM LEIBNITZ

Your Own Love Symbol

Choose a song, color, perfume, wine, or flower, and
make it "yours."

Share the intimacy and the belongingness of this every
time there is an occasion to do so. Share the love that
your "love symbol" expresses.

Your Own Love Code

Whenever you mail a letter or card to your loved one, have some special form of visible affection on it, such as addressing it to "The Delightful Miss ——."

Or add some other qualifying sign of how special she is:

—Have a special mark on the flap.
—Put the postage stamp on upside down, or sideways, or in a special corner of the envelope.

Work out a "love code" between you, and always use it.

Make Love News

In most cities, the local newspaper maintains a historical file. Usually they will either lend you a particular day's edition so that you can take it to be photostated, or they will make one for you.

Choose a special day—the day your loved one was born . . . the day of your meeting or engagement . . . some important personal day—and have the front page of the paper photostated and mounted, perhaps framed.

Present it to your love partner on the anniversary of that special date.

Music to Love By

There must be record albums, one or many, that appeal to you both and put you "in the mood." Whatever the music . . . Beethoven . . . George Gershwin . . . The Rascals . . . quietly agree that it is your "music to love by."

And when you want to relax, to be together, to be just for each other, you should make it a point to set up the phonograph (or tape recorder) and play your love concert.

A Loving Cup of Wine

Wine is perhaps the most popular and universal drink, and it comes in hundreds of varieties. Make it a love project to try different wines with your lover until you both find one that is especially pleasing.

Thereafter, make the wine of your choice the "loving cup" that you'll drink on special occasions.

> *Or leave a kiss within the cup,*
> *And I'll not ask for wine.*
> —BEN JONSON,
> *To Celia*

Dressed for Love

Dress for him. In all your wardrobe, there is one dress or ensemble that is especially becoming in your partner's eyes.

Wear this special outfit on special occasions, and tell your love you're doing it to help say "I love you."

Persian Love

This is an excursion that, with a little forethought, could be the most delightful time you two have ever spent together.

What you need is: your sweetheart, a loaf of bread, some wine, *and* either "The Rubáiyát of Omar Khayyám" or one of the books of prose-poetry by Kahlil Gibran (*The Prophet* is an excellent choice).

Go out into the country, have your simple picnic, and read of love to your lover.

> *I hold it true, whate'er befall;*
> *I feel it, when I sorrow most;*
> *'Tis better to have loved and lost*
> *Than never to have loved at all.*
> —ALFRED LORD TENNYSON,
> *In Memoriam,* XXVII

Warm Up to Love

There is something of the caveman in us all: firelight warms more than just our bodies.

If you're lucky enough to have a fireplace, or access to one, make it a romantic point to use the glow and warmth of a fire to rekindle love, and loving thoughts.

When there is an occasion, spend the time alone with your lover in front of a fire. Think of the joys of curling up in a blanket on the floor in front of the hearth, and falling asleep as the fire turns to embers and then ashes.

Cook Up a Love Dish

Can't boil water? Your toast looks like charcoal? Don't you believe it! You can learn to cook, and all we're suggesting is one dish.

(Incidentally, it isn't sissified to cook—the world's greatest cooks are men!) But, man or woman, why not go to cooking school, making arrangements beforehand to learn to make just *one* gourmet dish.

Whatever it is—and there are thousands to choose from —let it be something you know your lover relishes. Learn to cook it in secret. Then, at a special time, prepare the dish as a love surprise, and serve it garnished with affection.

Tune In to Love

A wise poet said, "If music be the food of love, play on . . ."

Sweet music (music that sounds sweet to your ears, and your sweetheart's) is whatever you two agree upon. It may be folk music, love ballads, or songs from Broadway musicals.

Suggestion: Choose a local radio station that features the kind of music that you both like. Make a point of tuning in that station to provide constant background love music, especially when you are both feeling romantic. (And if you can't rely on a station, or if there are too many commercial interruptions, use records or tape of the music you love.)

Champagne—Love on Ice

Even if you think it tastes funny, or if it tickles your nose or doesn't have enough wallop, keep champagne special for special times.

Think of the excitement of having the local wine merchant deliver a chilled bottle to your lover just a short while before you arrive. You might learn or invent a special toast to drink to with your loved one.

Wherever, Whenever, Say "I Love You"

Communing, or communicating, is the basic building material of lasting, satisfying love. People find this difficult to do—they are "tongue-tied" at times. But here's a way of expressing love when you and your sweetheart are apart.

Make a ritual, a binding agreement between you. Agree that on any night you two must be apart, both of you, at exactly 11 P.M., will stop whatever you are doing, look out a window at the sky (even if it's cloudy or raining) and make a wish upon a star. Or that at some prearranged time you'll stop whatever you are doing and think about each other.

If you make the agreement and stick to it, it becomes one of those shared experiences that you will enjoy talking about later.

> *Man's love is of man's life a thing apart,*
> *'Tis a woman's whole existence.*
>
> —LORD BYRON,
> *Don Juan,* I

෫෨෨෨෨

Love Is a Movie

The movies have depicted most of the great love stories of the ages. Some, like *Camille, Intermezzo,* and *An Affair to Remember,* have become classics.

Like any pleasant, shared experience, a romantic movie is something that can tie the bonds of love more tightly between the two of you. So when your favorite love story makes the circuit again, see it together, even if it's for the umpteenth time. (You'll find new facets to enjoy each time you see it.)

A Good Deal of Love

Playing cards go back centuries. They hold a magical spell for people, and there is much in the way of tricks, games, and "fortune-telling" that can be done with them.

Playing cards is one gentle pastime for sweethearts. Here's an idea to make it even more a way of communicating your fondness.

Obtain a good photo of your loved one. Have it enlarged (or reduced, as necessary), and very carefully paste it in over the picture of the Queen (or King) of Hearts. The other 51 cards remain the same. But the "love card" of the deck you use most often (for solitaire, or gin rummy, or whatever) now bears the likeness of your lover.

IF YOU ARE

female ... married ... still the

sweetheart of the man you married

... young in heart, thought, actions

... You'll find in this section

some wonderful ways to

tell him, often, that

he's special.

Love is so important, so universal, that Greeks had *two* words for it, not one. These words were *eros* and *agape*. *Eros* is romantic, emotional, and physical love between lovers, sweethearts, and husbands and wives. *Agape* means caring and sharing, being concerned.

So you see, love is not limited to physical attraction between man and woman. The expression of love is difficult—yet it is really so easy, so wanted, so welcome, that it should come to everyone as naturally as breathing.

It isn't difficult—in fact, it's easy to love one person, any one person, at any time. Relax and let yourself love!

The next time the feeling wells up within you, let it come out. Don't stifle it in your mind, or strangle it in your throat. Express the emotion, convey the feeling, and let your loved ones know that they are *special*.

Love That Grows and Grows

Grow something!

If you have a home with even a little bit of ground around it, make it a love ritual to plant a living, growing, green thing to commemorate a particular event.

Let it be the beginning of a little arbor of trees . . . or a rose bush (the first of many) . . . or a small evergreen bush. Choose the plant, or shrub, or seedling, and bring it home. Then, with your mate, plant it.

As it grows, let it remind you of your togetherness, and of your growing love.

Love is not a natural phenomenon. Passion is. Selfishness is. But love is something that must be cultivated.

—ROBERT E. MOORE

Something Nutty—But So Is Love

A loaf of bread . . . a jug of wine . . . all the rest of it brings to mind romantic visions of outdoor bliss.

But it isn't always possible to get away from it altogether. So why not beat the odds, and have a picnic at home.

What you need is a blanket spread on the floor, a transistor radio, and the same kind of fun food that you'd take on a picnic.

Use paper plates and napkins and all the other conveniences you would on a picnic. Forget fuss and formality, relax, and enjoy each other and the frivolity of doing something silly.

Where there's marriage without love, there will be love without marriage.

—BENJAMIN FRANKLIN,
Poor Richard's Almanack

Have a Love of Reading

It wasn't too long ago that the joy of reading united sweethearts. We suggest a revival of that lovely custom.

Read aloud to one another. Choose a poem, a short story, or a novel that both of you will enjoy. Set aside a quiet time, in a quiet place, and communicate (never mind that you are using someone else's words—the feeling is yours).

Try the magic of reading. It works wonders in knitting the love bonds between you.

The Scent of Love Is Everywhere

On an evening when you are feeling especially romantic, and when you want him to feel the same, carefully put a drop of your sexiest perfume (use a cotton swab, and use perfume, not cologne or toilet water) on each light bulb in the living room, or bedroom.

The heat of the bulb will cause the scent to permeate the air. It will smell heavenly!

If you would be loved,
love and be lovable.
—BENJAMIN FRANKLIN

One-Sheet Love

The one-sheet refers to the size of a normal poster (big roadside billboards are "24-sheeters").

In high school art classes there are undoubtedly some very talented young people who can express their artistic talents in many ways, including the popular poster form.

Our suggestion: Through the head of the art department, contact a talented youngster, and commission him or her to do a love poster.

It may only be the words "I love you" lettered in "psychedelic script"; it may be her name lettered over and over; it may be an intricate series of hearts surrounding the date on which you met.

Just give the artist two or three thoughts, and let him execute the poster.

Then have the poster mounted (use Masonite, or some other hardboard that isn't going to warp with humidity) and hang it in the den, rumpus room, or kitchen—someplace where your husband will see it often.

Stay Slim and Trim for Love

There is a line (probably untrue) that everybody loves a fat man.

But you don't hear that about bulging females. Even the "fat man" prefers his women slim and trim (but with curves in the right places!).

So use the wise combination of diet and exercise to keep yourself in trim, and to keep him in a passionate frame of mind.

Periodically, and with prudence, you might embark on a new diet (if your doctor approves) and tell him that you're going on a diet for love—to keep love alive!

> *Oh, rank is good, and gold is fair,*
> *And high and low mate ill;*
> *But love has never known a law*
> *Beyond its own sweet will!*
> *—JOHN GREENLEAF WHITTIER,*
> *Amy Wentworth*

A Love-ly Love Song

Surely your loved one has a special love song that means "it" just to him.

Be lavish and buy, as a surprise, a whole bunch of different recordings of the same song: instrumentals, solo singers, choral groups, every type.

Stack them on the automatic phonograph one evening, and start the machine going at the appropriate time.

Love by Subscription

Here's an inexpensive but thoughtful idea for a special gift, especially when budget is a problem.

Everybody has a "special interest." Consider getting a magazine subscription to fit that special interest. You'll find there is something published on every subject; your local librarian can be helpful in looking up the proper title in the periodicals index.

Then have a gift subscription mailed to your loved one. Better yet, buy one issue yourself and give it to him with a special note that the rest are coming on a regular basis. It will be a constant reminder of your consideration and thoughtfulness.

A Real Love Match

Here's an inexpensive idea that demonstrates thought and interest.

Every good stationery or department store can have special matchbooks made up to your order (just like printed Christmas cards) with almost any kind of "copy."

Why not order a batch saying "Tenth Anniversary," or "Happy Birthday (John)," and use them at the next party that signifies something for you both.

Or have some matchbooks made up just as his own personal supply to carry in pocket or wallet with "I love you," or any other kind of brief description or initials that mean something to you both.

Breathless Love

There are a dozen wonderful breath fresheners on the market today. They come in small, convenient sprays or bottles—and they work.

Slip one into the bedside table drawer, or under your pillow.

In the morning (or even during the night), use the product to wake up and freshen your breath, and then lean over and wake up your mate with a good-morning kiss.

*

Lace-y Love

Do something daring, and unexpected!

Whatever your normal choice of lingerie or sleepwear, there is something on the market that is a little more provocative, daring, revealing.

Some day soon, with no plan in mind, and no announcement, purchase this special piece of lingerie, and spring it as a surprise on your husband.

He'll be delighted!

All-Absorbing Love

Every January, and again in August, most department stores have white sales. They'd better, because this love thought can be costly!

Buy at least two or three of the biggest bath towels (the wrap-around kind that seems as large as a bedsheet), and have them monogrammed, appliquéd (or whatever) by the store with his initials or just the word HIS.

To make the towel a special memento of your love, don't detract from its uniqueness or importance by having matching towels for you. These super-towels should be for your sweetheart alone.

All other goods by Fortune's hand are given;
A wife is the peculiar gift of heaven.
— ALEXANDER POPE,
January and May

A Frame-Up for Love

There are talented, capable craftswomen all over the country. Ask around, among neighbors or friends or relatives, until you find through them a lady who embroiders or "samples."

Contact her and ask if she will make for you (and you should ask how much you may pay her for her work) a personal love "sampler." (These were the old-fashioned, cross-stitched, framed displays that used to decorate living rooms. "God Bless Our Home," they would say, or "Truth is Love," or similar homilies.)

Your love sampler should be worded simply, with a short, meaningful love message for him. Have it appropriately framed, and make a present of it on a special occasion.

A Fragrance of Love

Be specially sweet-smelling. Of all the perfumes you have, one must be his favorite.

Make this "your scent," wear it exclusively, and don't be sparing of its use. Pleasant, personal scents are among the nicest ways of reminding your special someone that you care.

Giving Reaps Rewards of Love

Love is giving, say many philosophers.

If this is true, isn't the idea of giving to a destitute or orphaned child one true way of giving together?

There are many organizations (Foster Parents Plan, Save-the-Children Federation, and so on) that regularly advertise in national magazines. They are seeking people with love and charity in their hearts, and a little (you'd be surprised *how* little) money to give each month.

You and your loved one, in effect, become the "parents" of an unfortunate child that needs help, a child here or abroad. You communicate with the child and he with you. And in loving and giving together to a youngster who lacks both the material and emotional necessities of life, your own love will grow and flower!

We are shaped and fashioned by what we love.
—JOHANN W. VON GOETHE

Light Up Your Love

Candlelight makes the world seem softer, lovelier, more gentle.

When the next occasion at home presents itself, add to the mood, the intimacy, the warmth, and the love by having just candlelight. It's inexpensive, and it does say "I love you."

Serve It—with Love

Should mountains be named only after the very famous? Should desserts commemorate only the rich and successful? How about that special someone? Doesn't he deserve notice—even if you're the only one who notices?

Think of the ingredients that your loved one likes especially. Tuna fish? Rice? Chestnuts? Tomatoes? Combine two or three of them into a new dish that you invent. Cook it (on the QT) once, twice, three times, to make sure it's right. Then name it . . . Tuna à la Robert . . . Rice, Onions, and Chicken à la William . . . and *serve* it, with love.

Love and you will be loved. All love is mathematically just, as much as the two sides of an equation.

—RALPH WALDO EMERSON

There is no greater invitation to love than loving first.

—SAINT AUGUSTINE

A Labor of Love

What do you do well? Sew? Bake? Garden?

Whatever hobby or handicraft it is, undertake a secret do-it-yourself project. Make something special for your loved one. Do it without his knowing it. Then, with love, give him your handiwork on a special, personal occasion.

Love Is Mutual

If you have children . . .

On each *child*'s birthday, give your husband a special, small, but loving gift.

After all, your children are a living memorial to your mutual love.

> *Never treat the worst those*
> *whom you love the best.*

Love Like Royalty

Loafing is not for the working man. To be a person of luxury takes money—or thoughtfulness.

You may not have the money, but you can always be considerate. Think about making a special day seem extra special by serving your sweetheart a breakfast tray in bed.

You should be able to arise a little early . . . to prepare breakfast quietly . . . to set a handsome tray with a flower or two in a vase and the newspaper or mail on it for relaxed reading . . . and then, waking your special man with a smile and declaring, "I love you," to serve breakfast in bed.

Do it again—next year, same day.

Decorating Your Love

Right after next Christmas—just before the stores put their holiday items away—go searching.

What you're looking for is a very special ornament —just one—that can have meaning only for the two of you.

Maybe it's the shape . . . or color . . . or maybe it's something you can have a florist (or a professional window decorator) make up. It should be different and personal.

Keep it hidden away until next Christmas. Then hang it on your tree, with a special holiday kiss and a statement of your love.

Each year, when you decorate your home for the holidays, renew your love with the "love ornament."

Love is eternal. The aspect may change, but not the essence. There is the same difference in a person before and after he is in love as there is in an unlighted lamp and one that is burning. The lamp was there and a good lamp, but now it is shedding light too, and that is its real function. And love makes one calmer about many things, and that way, one is more fit for one's work.

—VINCENT VAN GOGH

Make Up—with the Strength of Love

It's inevitable that you'll quarrel—you're human, aren't you? Pride is the brick and mortar that builds walls separating lovers. So never have the false pride that prevents you from being the first to say "I'm sorry" . . . "I didn't mean it" . . . "Let's make up."

Kisses are sweeter than tears. Smiles are better for your blood pressure than scowls. Don't think that "giving in" is a weakness. It's actually the strength of love that makes you want to make up.

To have and to hold from this day forward, for better, for worse, for richer, for poorer, in sickness and in health, to love and to cherish, 'til death do us part.

—*Book of Common Prayer*

❦❧❦❧❦❧

This Hidden Love Is Okay

Leave short, handwritten notes of affection (composed by you) around the house . . . under a pillow . . . in a drawer . . . behind a book . . . anywhere.

Arrange with your husband's secretary (or a co-worker) to "plant" these notes in places where the man in your life will find them on the job.

How to Shop for Love

In the "shop by mail" sections of many of the women's magazines, you'll find advertisements for personalized plates. These hand-painted plates are designed for display, not for use.

On them are painted such things as name, birth date, astrological sign, flower or birthstone, and so on. They are not terribly expensive and they are handsome and personal.

Send for one, or maybe a pair—one for your sweetheart and one for yourself—and give them as a token of love. Make sure there is a place, a prominent place, where the plates can hang to "show off" your affection.

Make a Hobby of Love

Make something together. There are kits that you can buy to make hooked rugs . . . you can learn to refinish furniture very simply . . . it's easy to install self-adhesive floor tiles.

Whatever you can do together that needs doing in your home, make it a joint project. But don't be bossy. Make it a true partnership effort, and show your love by sharing the planning, the drudgery, and the satisfaction of doing it jointly.

Then, whenever you use or enjoy what you've made, comment on it as a reminder of your mutual affection.

Stop It! I Love You!

What do you do that irritates your partner?

Leave the cap off the toothpaste tube? Spill bobby pins on the table? Forget to have the gas tank filled each time you use the car?

Identify your spouse's pet peeve and stop doing it! But instead of making this a negative value, make it positive. Each and every time you show your consideration by not doing the thing that outrages your husband, leave a note that says in effect, "I didn't, because I love you."

A Stitch in Time Says Love

Can you cross-stitch?

Whatever form of stitching you can master, think of converting that skill into a visible, tangible mark of your emotion.

Make a sampler:

Bless My Love—A. B.
Be My Love—C. D.
Always—E. F.

Some simple, similar sentiment, permanently stitched and framed for the wall, makes a lovely gift, a lovely remembrance, a constant reminder.

❦❦❦

Love Letters

Use the mails! Send a short letter, or a poem, or a store-bought card to your husband at his place of work. He'll remember how much he loves you!

Share Your Love-ly Memories

A popular Broadway show had as its title song *The Happy Time*. That's what the objective of life is: Happiness.

There is no surer way to reinforce your love than to relive happy times with your loved one. Little children love to hear favorite, pleasant stories told and retold. So do adults.

Pick a quiet time. Sit with a glass of wine or a favorite beverage, and the two of you will go off in reveries. Remember the time that . . .

Think about, talk about, share a happy time of the past. In doing so, you'll brighten your todays and grow close once again, as you mentally and emotionally relive your happy yesterdays.

Choose a Special "Loving Place"

It can be a secluded parking spot . . . a favorite booth in a restaurant . . . a cozy nook in your home . . . a place under the trees in your yard. But make it a place that is free from care and worry . . . where tenderness and love are the only "outsiders" that you and your loved one allow to enter.

Make it a point to keep the place special . . . and when there are hard times, when the world is a little strained, go to your loving place and enjoy just being with each other.

The language that God hears best is the silent language of love.

—SAINT JOHN OF THE CROSS

Love That Message

You can make a magic message appear in your home. Here are some ideas—all of which should be used to convey a love message:

1. Write a love message on the bathroom mirror with a sliver of soap. Then, when the mirror steams up (from a shower or bath) the soaped letters will *not* carry the condensation, and the message will show up.
2. On the inside of Venetian blind slats, cutting across several of them, write a message in some material—finger paint will do—that will easily wash off. (Don't use a Magic Marker or a pen. Use some other writing implement.) Write the message with the blind closed. Next open the blind so that the slats are horizontal. Than, when the slats are tipped closed, the message will show up.
3. Use an aerosol can of pre-mixed whipped cream as your "pen." Write a love message on the top of a cake or pie; make a heart on the surface of a cup of coffee; decorate any food with a heart, or initials, or I.L.Y.

Use your imagination for simple surprises that tell your sweetheart just how you feel.

≈≈≈≈

Falling in Love Again

For married folks only . . .

If you had to do it all over, would you? If the answer is "yes," always "yes," for both of you, then why not do it all over again?

Why not re-marry? Why not take the same vows (now with a different, deeper meaning) and become once again man and wife " 'til death do you part"?

What surer way of saying "I love you!"

Do not be afraid of showing affection. Be warm and tender, thoughtful and affectionate. Men are more helped by sympathy than by service. Love is more than money, and a kind word will give more pleasure than a present.
—JOHN LUBBOCK

≈≈≈≈

IF YOU ARE

male ... married and glad of it ...;

loving but perhaps occasionally.

forgetful ... and you know she is

the only girl in the world for you

... Then invest time and effort

in some of these ways.

OVER the years it has been our experience that women never tire of hearing, or being shown, that they are loved. Over and over they want to be told. Each time they react with the joy and wonder of the first time.

Your wife has been, always, the only woman you love, and you are still her sweetheart. But you've been tongue-tied about affection for years. How do you let her know of your love? On the following pages there are some suggestions for you: gestures for no particular reason except to show her spontaneously that you love her; gifts, and how to make them thoughtful; and special occasions, and the importance of being personal about them, especially if the sky's the limit.

Here are some daily thoughts and ideas about little gifts for no special occasion. Try these little "kindness activities" to *show* her how you feel:

Remember—little things mean a lot!

Make Your Love a Headliner

Many amusement parks and novelty stores and some mail-order houses will make up a dummy newspaper with a special big headline to your order.

Have one of these made to say:

WILSONS NAMED LOVINGEST COUPLE

or

GREENS' BLISS LASTS EIGHT YEARS

or some other short, personal message.

Arrange with your newsboy to "tack" this phony newspaper on to the front page of the real, local newspaper he delivers, and make sure your loved one sees it first!

෫෮ඁ෮ඁ෮

Make Love Pop Up

For the nimble-fingered, only . . .

Most facial tissues are interfolded. When you pull one out, the next one pops up. You can make a love note pop up too, with a little careful work.

This involves, first of all, writing a selection of love notes on small slips of paper. Then carefully insert one of these into the fold of the stack of tissues, working from the top down. (This obviously works best if the tissues have been taken out of their cardboard box, and are in a dispenser.)

If you do your job meticulously, a love note will pop up when the tissues are pulled. (Don't try to do a whole box, just sprinkle a dozen or so throughout the pack.)

∽∾∽∾∽∾

A Love Message

When the bathroom mirror is steamed over (from a hot shower or bath), use it as a place to write a quick love message. Get out of the bathroom, and persuade your loved one to go in to see your message.

(You can also use a frosted-over window at home or in the car in winter.)

Love on Account

Unbeknown to your loved one, open up a special savings account in her name. Regularly, every week or every month —but *regularly*—deposit a fixed amount in it, whatever you can afford.

Then, at the end of a year, there will be about $50 (assuming you've been putting away a dollar a week), or $100, or more.

Make a gift of the passbook to your loved one, with a note that says: "Because I love you, I want you to have this to do whatever you please with—no matter how kooky, unnecessary, or frivolous it may be."

Honeymoon for "Old" Lovers

If you've been married for any length of time, undoubtedly you tend to idealize your honeymoon. It might have been fine, and then again, it might not have been. After all, you both were tense . . . unsure . . . new at the relationship. So do it all over again.

Make arrangements at a local or nearby hotel or resort for a weekend for just the two of you. Arrange for someone to look after the children.

Then, take off for the weekend away from it all. You'll renew your love with this affectionate escape.

Don't Fight for Love

Disagreements and arguments usually start with some-one's hurt ego. If yours is involved, okay, fine. But remember, women have far greater sensibilities than men.

Isn't there something you do that she would like done differently? Stop and think. What is it . . . the way you part your hair? . . . the way you leave your clothes strewn about? . . . careless driving?

Whatever you do that bothers your mate, discipline yourself, and change. And tell her you've changed because you love her.

There is nothing which cannot be borne with cheerful alacrity by those who love one another.

—SAINT THERESA

⟅⟅⟅⟅⟅⟅

A Love-ly Plaque

In every city and town there are still skilled men and women who work with their hands. Think about having a woodcarving made to express your love. Visit your local high school, and ask the manual training instructor if he knows a woodcarver—he usually will.

Phone or visit this craftsman, and tell him you want a decorative plaque or wall decoration that will express some of your love.

Tell him about your loved one, the things and experiences that you've shared and enjoyed. Then let his creative tools make a permanent reminder of your affection. When it's done, make a special present of it to her.

A Sterling Way to Say "I Love You"

Why not start a silver collection for your wife? It can be anything, a silver goblet, an antique cosmetic jar, a candlestick, anything that you can find a piece at a time in the thrift or antique shops in your city.

The idea is to give one piece on a particular day, and then do the same annually thereafter. Maybe it's for Mother's Day, or a birthday, or such. The idea is to make the collection grow; even though the pieces don't match, who cares? They are individually lovely, and each has value. But don't buy silver plate; buy sterling.

Have a Love-ly Weekend

Give your loved one a "vacation at home."

Plan a weekend (or a week, if you have the time off) in which you do everything that your mate wants and likes.

Fix breakfast in bed for her. Arrange for the children to be taken care of. Lunch out. Go to a concert or on a picnic.

No work . . . no worries . . . no monotonous chores. At the beginning and end of each day, tell your mate, "This is your day, because I love you."

The best portion of a good man's life is his nameless, unremembered acts of kindness and love.

—WILLIAM WORDSWORTH

Love, by Any Other Name

What is your most prized possession?

Car . . . boat . . . house? Why not name it after your loved one?

It isn't very expensive, and certainly need not be ostentatious to have a simple hand-lettered name applied to the prow or hood, or to have a small sign made for the front of your home.

This sign says, implicitly: "My most prized possession is named in honor of my beloved."

Make a Sacrifice for Love

The heroine in the movies often says, "If you really loved me, you'd . . ."

What is meant is, you would give up something. In other words, you would sacrifice.

The tone is unpleasant and the attitude is wrong, but the point is right! If you do love someone truly, you are prepared to give up something.

Maybe it's watching pro football all weekend long. Perhaps your wife would be happier if you didn't drive over 50 miles per hour or didn't eat onions on your hamburger. Whatever it may be, there is surely something that you could stop doing that would please your loved one.

Think about it. Select something. Give it up. And tell your wife you've done it just for her.

❧❧❧

Faith Is Love

Elsewhere we've said, "God is Love." That is a universal truth.

In these tense, troubled times, more and more people are returning to God and formal religion.

Think about the togetherness of worshiping together—at the church or temple of your faith. And do it regularly (with your children, if you have any).

The slogan, "The family that prays together stays together," is far more than just words.

$\infty\infty\infty\infty$

Love Letters

Send a note, a poem, or a pretty greeting card to your wife at home. Normally, she will receive the mail when you are not at home, and this will be a special, unexpected, surprising way of saying how you feel toward her.

A Kiss—the Salute of Love

Never part without a kiss!

A kiss seals the affection between you. A kiss is the gentlest, sweetest way of reminding your sweetheart that she is your loved one.

When you leave home for a day at work . . . when you go fishing or golfing . . . when you go on a business trip . . . when you "part" to go to sleep . . . whenever you won't be together for a long or short interval (and no matter how strained your immediate relationship may be before the parting), make it a never-failing rule to say "I love you" with your lips. Kiss her now!

A new Commandment I give unto you. That you love one another; as I have loved you, that you also love one another.

—*Saint John,* 13: 34

A First Prize for Love

Give a trophy to your special person. In card and gift shops, you can buy trophies like the little tiny "toy" ones, usually silver-colored plastic or glass, with a printed label or a blank that you can hand-letter. Or go all the way and purchase one at a silver or jewelry store.

The "loving cup" (as they are often called) can be actually engraved with a particular, personal message, one that is special to both of you. For instance:

"World's Best Spaghetti-Sauce Cook"
"Champion Saturday Spouse"
"1st Place, Southern States Annual Kissing Contest"
"Winner, National Sweethearts Meet"

You can put a date on it to add to its special nature. Present it on an important occasion.

Love Has a Special Ring to It

In days of old the ring finger of the left hand was thought to have a direct connection to the heart. That is why engagement rings are placed on the third finger of the left hand, and why wedding bands also grace that finger.

Whatever the design or price of your wedding band, it was probably less costly than one you could afford today. So, on a special wedding anniversary, express your continuing love with another wedding ring—fancier . . . more expensive . . . but no less loving than the original.

Dish Up Some Love

It's an old saying: "A woman's work is never done." Household drudgery can sometimes make her feel less like a desirable female than like a scullery maid.

Some evening after a particularly strenuous day for her, clear the table after dinner, do the dishes, put away things.

Don't volunteer, don't hint at it, just do it. And keep doing it occasionally. Then, instead of rushing to the television set or picking up the paper, set out two brandies for a romantic after-dinner drink.

Plant a Patch of Love

Do you have a green thumb, and a patch of ground? If so, there is no more verdant way to remind her of your affection than to plant a flower bed, or cultivate some shrubs, or put down a plot of good, green grass that "says something."

For example, the flower bed could be in the shape of a heart, or of your loved one's initials. (It may not be readily apparent to others, but the two of you will know it's there.) Similarly, shrubs and bushes can be planted in the same manner, or trimmed to a particular shape or in the form of letters. And planting part of the lawn area in a special, dense (or different-colored green) grass can say the same thing.

The wonderful part is that this expression of love keeps on growing.

❧❧❧

A Reflection of Love

You can make a big hit and show your inventive genius at the same time by installing a "rear-view" mirror in the bathroom so it will be easier for her to do her hair.

Just get an inexpensive mirror in the five-and-ten-cent store and hang it directly opposite the existing mirror on your medicine cabinet. This way she can see both the front and back of her head when combing and brushing.

There's not a female in the world who won't appreciate this little do-it-yourself task.

*   *   *

A Puzzle Solved Is Love

For a clever and highly personal anniversary present, take your wedding picture to a photography shop and have an enlargement made, at least 10 by 12 inches. Tell the photographer you want it mounted (glued down) on ⅛-inch cardboard backing.

Then carefully cut the enlargement apart into jigsaw puzzle shapes, present it to her in a gift box, and let her assemble it.

Enclose a note saying, "It's nice to be together."

Love for the Road

Women like to be feminine at all times. That means they have to have little conveniences like mirrors, combs, lipsticks, and so on, always handy. Why not show your consideration by making the family car (usually a man's province) more comfortable for your loved one by providing some of the female appurtenances?

You can get many kinds of mirrors for the sun visor; you can have a tissue dispenser installed inexpensively; there are also car vanities available that are compartmentalized for things like make-up, comb, brush, and tissue disposal.

Surprise her one day with this equipment and watch her eyes light up with affection and appreciation.

ↄ৩ↄ৩ↄ৩৩

That Wonderful Year of Love

ASCAP (American Society of Composers, Authors, and Publishers, 575 Madison Avenue, New York, N. Y. 10022) has put out several listings of the top songs over the years. One volume is top Broadway show tunes, 1917–1957, and there are others.

Get such a list, and through the cooperation of a local record store and a recording studio, make up a "wonderful year" record for your sweetheart. On it, have recorded ten, twenty, or thirty of the most popular songs of your special year (when you met, were married, whatever). Have a label made for it, and present it on an anniversary.

೭ঌ৩ঌ৩

Related to Love

Never mind those stale jokes about mothers-in-law.

Every girl feels flattered when her lover pays attention to and shows consideration for her mother.

Why not send your mother-in-law flowers or a box of candy once in a while, with a specially appropriate note of affection?

Your spouse will love you for it, and her mother will tell daughter repeatedly what a lucky girl she is to have found you.

❧❧❧

Time Out for Love

Are you a weekend golfer, a pro-football fan, or do you reserve a day or night out with "the boys"?

She might appreciate it and think you extra-special if you take time out during half-time, or between poker hands, and call her up to see how her day or evening is progressing.

It shows that even when pursuing your own interests, you care about her when she's alone.

Let Your Love Grow

Man is an acquisitive animal; he loves to collect things (and so do women!).

You can mark your affection and show your sweetheart how your affection grows by collecting for her. One beautiful way is with a simple pearl (real, not simulated or artificial) necklace.

You start with a clasp and a single pearl; then add pearls on every occasion that you want to say, "I love you." Nearly any good jeweler will be delighted to undertake such a project with you, and will have the proper pearls available, graduated according to size, for the "love telling" occasions you wish.

Every time you add a pearl to her necklace, make sure that there is a card or a note that says something personal to accompany the bauble.

❧❧❧

A Love Song Made to Order

Many public places, restaurants, night clubs, even bars and lounges, have orchestras or small music groups.

Most of these are fairly proficient at "faking it" (playing a song that they don't really know, or for which they don't have the music).

What you can do, the very next time you and your loved one are going to such a place, is to make arrangements in advance with the musical group leader for them to play "your song" when you come into the place, or at a special time.

It is easy, working with the owner, the maître d'hôtel, or the captain of waiters, to develop a signal that will cue the music.

It should prove a memorable occasion—for both of you.

What are our two needs? Someone to love us—someone for us to love.

Flower Power

It may sound extravagant, but isn't your love partner worth a flower a day?

What sweeter way to say "I love you" than with flowers? Just a single blossom, and it needn't be an expensive American Beauty rose that conveys your message.

The important thing is to mark a month (or week) or other period of time, with a fresh posy each day. Pick it out at the florist, and deliver it yourself.

(Tip: If you tell the florist in advance what you plan to do, you can usually buy the flowers **on** a continuing basis at a special money-saving price.)

Love is the master key that opens
the gates of happiness.

∽∞∽∞∽

How to Say

"I LOVE YOU"

From A to Z

How to Say "I Love You"—from A to Z

COUNTRY	LANGUAGE	WORDS	PHONETIC ENGLISH PRONUNCIATION
Afghanistan	Pashto	بر ته ښ م	Za ta sara maina larum
China	Cantonese	我爱你	Wo-ai-nee
Denmark	Danish	JEG ELSKER DIG	Yi aelskah di
Estonia	Estonian	MINA ARMASTAN SIND	Meena arma stan seend
Finland	Finnish	MINÄ RAKASTAN SINUA	Mena ra'kastan si'nua
France	French	JE T'AIME	Je t'em
Germany	German	ICH LIEBE DICH	Ish leeba dish
Greece	Greek	Σ'ΑΓΑΠΩ	Saga po'
Hungary	Hungarian	SZERETLEK	Se-ret-lek
Iceland	Icelandic	Eg elska þig	Egh elska thig

COUNTRY	LANGUAGE	WORDS	PHONETIC ENGLISH PRONUNCIATION
Indonesia	Indonesian	AKU TJINTA PADAMU	Ah'kooh Tcheehm'tah Pah'dah'mooh
Iran	Persian	تُرا دوست دارم	Tora dost dáram
Israel	Hebrew	אֲנִי אוֹהֵב אוֹתְךָ	Ahnee ohev otcha (to a boy)
		אֲנִי אוֹהֵב אוֹתָךְ	Ahnee ohev otach (to a girl)
Italy	Italian	TI AMO	Tee-ah-maw
Japan	Japanese	貴方が大好	Anata dai'suki
Latvia	Latvian	ES MĪLU TEVI	Es mee'loo te vih
Yiddish	Yiddish	איך האָב דיך ליב	Yikh hub dikh leeb

How to Say "I Love You"—from A to Z

COUNTRY	LANGUAGE	WORDS	PHONETIC ENGLISH PRONUNCIATION
Lithuania	Lithuanian	AŠ MYLIU TAVE	Ush mee'loo ta veh
Netherlands	Dutch	IK HOU VAN JOU	Ik how vahn jow
Norway	Norwegian	JEG ELSKER DEG	Ai elska day
Pakistan	Pakistanian		Muje se mu habbat hai
Poland	Polish	JACIE KOCHAM	Ya'cha kocham
Portugal	Portuguese	AMO-TE	Ah moo te
Rumania	Rumanian	TE IU BESC	Teh you besk
Russia	Russian	Я ЛЮБЛЮ ВАС	Ya liubliu' vas
Spain	Spanish	YO TE AMO	Eo te ahmo

COUNTRY	LANGUAGE	WORDS	PHONETIC ENGLISH PRONUNCIATION
Tunisia	Tunisian	*(Arabic script)*	Ha eh bak
Turkey	Turkish	SENI SEVIYORUM	Seni sevi yorum
Yugoslavia	Yugoslavian	JA TE VOLIM	Ya teh volym
Zambia	Cinyanja	NDI KU KONDA	N'di koo konda
	Silozi	NA KULATA	Na ku lata
	Tonga	NDA KUYANDA	N'da koo yanda